The Proverbs of Hell Explained
Written by Jonathan Charles Doyle

ISBN 978-0-578-13060-6

"The Proverbs of Hell Explained"
Copyright Jonathan Charles Doyle 2013

Legends of Monadnock Printing Press 2013

2nd Edition "Marshmallow Chips" Version

Illustrations created by Jonathan Doyle
Using proprietary photo editing technique.

Contact: legendsofmonadnock@gmail.com

Marshmallow Chips

"The sweetest chip with the saltiest flavor"

THE PROVERBS OF HELL EXPLAINED

Written by
Jonathan Charles Doyle

Preface

This book was created with a formula in mind. The formula is this:

Creativity + Explanations + Simplicity + Genuine attempt to understand − Lofty pretension = The Proverbs of Hell Explained

I humbly admit that a deeper more in depth exploration of "The Proverbs of Hell" with broader reaching explanations would be most appropriate for explaining this great work.

I have labored for 3 years just to provide readers with my own interpretations. I hope they are helpful but cannot tell you they are correct.

This book is not just a boring exegesis. It is also a fun journey to be experienced. May your experience of this book awaken parts of your own vision of this world.

Marshmallow Chips − *" The Sweetest Chip With the Saltiest Flavor"*

Acknowledgments

There have been a few wonderful individuals who have commented on and critiqued my humble attempt for interpreting "The Proverbs of Hell".

Though the entirety of this book is my responsibility, it does warrant acknowledgments.

Alex Gutterman - A good friend of mine, took the time to look through all that I had generated for text and concept. He provided key insights for a few of the proverbs and improved the already developed concepts for several of the proverbs.

Geloey Galadrielle – This fine woman went through the entire manuscript to make sure that the grammar was correct. She was also very supportive as a friend during the final months of the books completion.

Robert Emmett Kelly- A supportive friend who had some key insights for a few proverbs and helped develop a few others through critique and supportive motivation.

Introduction

Welcome to Jonathan Doyle's guided tour through William Blake's Proverbs of Hell. This little volume packs a big punch, inviting us to expand our capacities, stretch our imaginations, and challenge our assumptions.

Many great mystics, wisdom traditions, and spiritual teachers throughout history have pointed us in a direction towards integration of "opposites" in our consciousness. They have asserted that the human mind cripples itself when it breaks this glorious Universe of experience up into categories, when it cordons off entire realms of thought, affect, and activity and, through slavishness to habits of thinking and behavior, smugly attaches itself to one side or other of the arbitrary fence. Buddhists talk about the importance of removing preference and revulsion, Nietzsche warned us against a thoughtless and small minded morality, Taoists look to the dark inside the light, Christ reminded us that Kingdom of Heaven is not accessible to those who haven't unified the male and female within themselves.
Blake was likely working in the same spirit

Marshmallow Chips – *" The Sweetest Chip With the Saltiest Flavor"*

when he penned the Proverbs, likely offering up these small jewels of thought, word, and emotion to help tease his readers into an adventure through themselves and their experiences, which adventure might, if the book was effective, help them shake petty, old, and limiting habits of first dividing the world from some small minded position, and then forever fencing off entire sections of that division, labeling one side as "good/heavenly" and the other as "bad/hellish".

In his Proverbs of Hell Explained, Doyle has taken what might appear to be a forbidding literary monolith of the past and worked to provide exegesis (and attractive illustrations) for each of Blake's pithy aphorisms and remarks that create a tone of everyday friendliness and straightforwardness. The effect is, and the gustatory analogy in the packaging brings home the point, to make the Proverbs, tasty, manageable to bite into, digestible, and above all, enjoyable. But don't think that in so doing Doyle loses sight of the depth and seriousness that are as much a part of the Proverbs as its humour. Hardly. The perhaps sometimes bitter pill of Wisdom is simply being coated with a more readily consumed outer shell. It's been my experience in exploring the Proverbs that once the pill is swallowed, so to speak, it does its work regardless of the sweetness of its coating.

This book has been a labour of Love for Jonathan, and it represents the sincere and focused attempt of his effort to get at the heart of Blake's great work. It has been both an honour and a pleasure to lend a small hand to Jonathan in discussing the Proverbs and their meanings. I have found myself alternately amused by, informed by, disagreeing with, and impressed by, the unique and characteristically whimsical ways that Jonathan approaches the text, and the examples and stories he gives to elucidate it. I also know that, attracted to Blake's thinking by this wonderfully entertaining yet subtle adventure through the Proverbs, I have received a nudge down the road of Wisdom referred to when I began this brief introduction.
Perhaps you will too.

Alexander Palache Gutterman
           Duluth, MN 11/13

Marshmallow Chips – "*The Sweetest Chip With the Saltiest Flavor*"

Table of Contents

In seed Time Learn, In harvest teach, In winter enjoy............2

Drive your cart and plow over the bones of dead............5

The road of excess leads to the palace of wisdom............7

Prudence is a rich ugly old maid courted by incapacity............9

He who desires but acts not breeds pestilence............11

The cut worm forgives the plow............13

Dip him in the river who loves water............17

A fool sees not the same tree a wise man sees............19

He whose face gives no light shall never become a star............21

Eternity is in love with the productions of time............23

The busy bee has no time for sorrow............25

Marshmallow Chips – "*The Sweetest Chip With the Saltiest Flavor*"

The hours of folly are measured by the clock, but of wisdom: no clock can measure...........27

All wholesome food is caught without a net or a trap..........................29

Bring out number weight and measure in year of dearth............................31

No bird soars to high if he soars with his own wings...........................33

A dead body revenges not injuries................35

The most sublime act is to set another before you...............................26

If the fool would persist in his folly he would become wise..................40

Folly is the cloak of knavery........................42

Shame is prides cloak................................44

Prisons are built with stones of law, Brothels with bricks of religion......................46

The Pride of the peacock is the glory of God...............................48

The lust of the goat is the bounty of God........50

The wrath of the lion is the wisdom of God..........52

The nakedness of woman is the work of God..........54

Excess of sorrow laughs, Excess of joy weeps..........56

The roaring of lions, the howling of wolves, the raging of the stormy sea, and the destructive sword, are portions of eternity too great for the eye of man..........60

The fox condemns the trap not himself..........62

Joy impregnates. Sorrows bring forth..........64

Let man wear the fell of a lion and the fleece of a sheep..........66

The bird a nest, the spider a web, man friendship..........68

The selfish smiling fool, & the sullen frowning fool, shall be both thought wise, that they may be a rod..........70

What is now proved was once only imagined..........72

Marshmallow Chips – *" The Sweetest Chip With the Saltiest Flavor"*

The rat, the mouse, the fox, the rabbit: watch the roots; the lion, the tiger, the horse, the elephant, watch the fruits..................74

The cistern contains; the fountain overflows..................76

One thought fills immensity..................78

Always be ready to speak your mind and a base man will avoid you..................80

Everything Possible to be believed is an image of truth..................83

The eagle never lost so much time as to learn of the crow..................86

The fox provides for himself, but God provides for the lion..................88

Think in the morning. Act in the noon. Eat in the evening. Sleep in the night..................90

He who has suffered you to impose on him knows you..................92

As the plow follows words, so God rewards prayers..................94

The tyger of wrath are wiser than the horse of instruction..................96

Expect poison from standing water............98

You never know what is enough unless you know what is more than enough..................100

Listen to the fools reproach it is a kingly title..102

The eyes of fire, the nostrils of air, the mouth of water, the beard of earth..104

The weak in courage are strong in cunning..107

The apple tree never asks the beech tree how he shall grow, nor the lion, the horse, how he shall take his prey..109

The thankful receiver bears a plentiful harvest..111

If others had not been foolish we should be so..113

The soul of sweet delight can never be defiled..116

When thou seest an eagle, thou seest a portion of genius, lift up thy head................119

Marshmallow Chips – "*The Sweetest Chip With the Saltiest Flavor*"

As the caterpillar chooses the fairest leaves to lay her eggs on, so the priest lays his curse on the fairest joys..............................121

To create a little flower is the labor of ages..............................123

Damn braces: Bless relaxes......................125

The best wine is the oldest the best water the newest..............................127

Prayers plow not! Sorrows weep not...........132

The head sublime, the heart pathos, the genitals beauty, the hands & feet proportion..............................134

As the air to a bird of the sea to a fish, so is contempt to the contemptible....................136

The crow wished everything was black, the owl everything was white.................................140

Exuberance is beauty................................142

If the lion was advised by the fox he would be cunning..............................144

Improvements makes straight roads, but the crooked roads without improvement are the roads of genius..............................146

Sooner murder an infant in its cradle then nurse unacted desires............149

Where man is not nature is barren............153

Truth can never be told so as to be understood, and not believed............154

Enough! Or too Much!............156

Marshmallow Chips – " *The Sweetest Chip With the Saltiest Flavor"*

"Marriage of Heaven and Hell"

I am sharing my interpretation of these proverbs, written by William Blake, to build a modern language/concept bridge to the meaning of this important work for the people of today. This precious wisdom gifted to us from William Blake is inspiring and fulfilling to the human experience when grasped with reverence. It is my hope that this book will help the modern reader find such reverence for the original text .

The book follows a simple format. I first present the reader with Blake's original text (in Italics), and then follow with my exegesis.

The Proverbs of Hell
-*William Blake*

In seed time learn, in harvest teach, in winter enjoy.

–William Blake

(I am illustrating this specific proverb in the "arc" of a single human lifetime and the changes that occur within this given lifetime. This Proverb can be seen as a fractal applicable to many different scenarios.)

-"In seed time learn" This represents the beginning of your life when you are asking a lot of questions and experiencing the world in a fresh way, ready to learn everything. On average this most likely represents the first 20-30 years of your life.

-"In Harvest teach" Harvest is the second phase of this three phase design. By this time you have learned a great deal from the first phase "In seed time learn". Having acquired a certain level of mastery of the first phase it is now your turn to teach all that you have discovered from your experiences and studies/reflections etc.

-"In winter enjoy" The final stage of your

life is meant to be enjoyed. You have endured the laborious tasks of both learning and teaching. Now it is time for you to hang and chill in the solar swing that is our galaxy with the infinite wisdom of all your experience.

Our Solar System

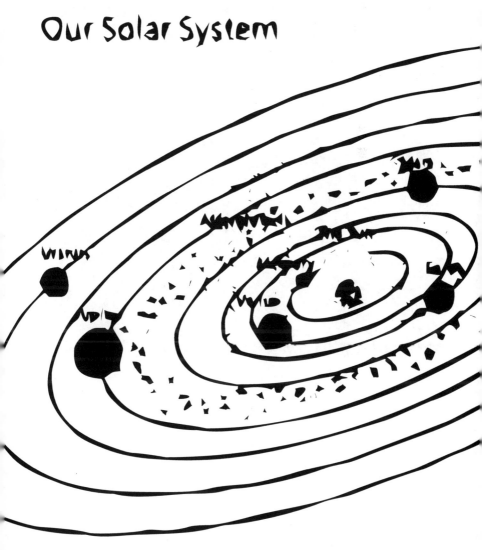

Marshmallow Chips – *"The Sweetest Chip With the Saltiest Flavor"*

Drive your cart and plow over the bones of the dead.

—William Blake

You should live for today and make your mark in the world over all the people who have come before you. Your own work is a product of all that came before you. The plow tills the soil of the past works and turns them over recycling the old into the new.

Example: Newton and Galileo believed that time worked in a linear chronologically fixed design and was the same for everyone. Then Einstein came along and brought us the theory of relativity, which is our modern view of time. Einstein's theory states that rates of time are different depending on relative motion. This is Einstein driving his cart and plowing over the bones of the dead.

Marshmallow Chips —" The Sweetest Chip With the Saltiest Flavor"

> *The road of excess leads to the palace of wisdom.*
>
> −William Blake

If you continually repeat an action or activity in your life you will become wise to the nature of what you are doing.

Example: If you study day and night learning how to play a video game and how to beat all the levels you become wise to all the intricacies of the game. You have played enough to know what you should and should not do. Where all the secret levels and bonuses are. The palace of wisdom is reached for this specific game by playing it endlessly until you have discovered its matrix thoroughly.

Prudence is a rich ugly old maid courted by incapacity.

−William Blake

Worrying, being too cautious or over-thinking about anything can make you well prepared for some things but can also make you inhibited and incapable of achieving goals or aims.

Example: Well if I go out, I might meet a girl, but we might even hit it off but her dad won't like me, and maybe her old boyfriend might assault me, and her dog will piss on my leg.

*Example contributed by Rick Spisak - He is a Blake enthusiast!

> *He who desires but acts not, breeds pestilence.*
>
> —William Blake

If you have desires that you are not acting on, they will create a disease or epidemic in your mind or being. This will happen because instead of finding an honest, healthy expression, they will come out in a twisted and indirect manner.

Example: A young girl (16 years old) grows up in a strict household and her parents watch her very closely and don't let her go out with her friends too long. The girl is sheltered by her parents' strictness. She goes to school and dreams about all the boys she really likes but is too afraid to get to know one because her mother and father might freak out and punish her for possibly being sexual with a boy. The parents are so afraid that their reputation in the community might get hurt if their daughter becomes pregnant or earns a "bad reputation".

The daughter is now 18 and free of her parents' parental grip. She now feels a powerful drive to have sex with everyone, even strangers at random. Her sexuality is now disconnected from the sincere needs of her heart. She is considered a nymphomaniac. Her mind and life have become diseased because she was unable to follow her natural desires and develop her understandings of intimacy in the precious years of her early teens.

The cut worm forgives the plow.

—William Blake

There are a lot of worms in the earth. When the farmer plows his field he cuts many worms in the process of creating his new crop. There is nothing the worms could do to prevent this. To the worm this is an act of God and so there is no one to blame and the worm must forgive this sad event.

Also the farmer's accidental destruction of the worm, though it is horrible, from a broader vantage point it is a constructive act of God to create an amazing crop. In fact, if you think about it, the worm's decomposing body even plays a part in helping the crop grow.

Example: Let's say you are living in Florida and there are major storm warnings. The storms come through your town and destroy your house and kill your pet dog. The force of nature, which no one has control over, has just overcome you. This is similar to the farmer's plow driving through the earth in the field cutting worms. In this scenario you are the worm that the storm (plow) came through and cut. This is something that you have to consider an "act of God" and you can blame no one, so therefore you must forgive the situation and accept it for what it is.

But look! Now a lot of unemployed people are being paid to help clean up and many people

who took life for granted have a renewed faith in the value of their own lives because they had such a close brush with death.

The community comes together seeing that the fences that divided all of their properties are really just fences and at the heart of the truth we are there for each other.

Without Gods plow this fact might not have been discovered by the worms.

Dip him in the river who loves water.

–William Blake

If you have fallen in love with a subject, person, place or thing,(not necessarily a noun...lol) then you should be submersed in that thing that brings you joy. The outcome from this action can yield extraordinary results.

Example: Mozart loved music from an early age. His father provided him with the environment to play music for his whole childhood. His father dipped him in that which he loved. And Now Mozart is a legend!

Marshmallow Chips –*" The Sweetest Chip With the Saltiest Flavor"*

A fool sees not the same tree that the wise man sees.

−William Blake

The fool sees a tree and knows little beyond this fact. The wise man sees the type of wood and its many different uses, whether it is dying and what kind of conditions it may thrive in, whether or not it has been diseased. He is even capable of knowing a drought is coming because the tree's leaves are wilting, etc. From understanding one tree, it may even be possible for the wise person to know the whole world and all of life.

Example: When you go to a used car lot and test-drive a vehicle you may be of the mind to appreciate the color of the paint or whether it has a leather interior. Let us also say that you are a person with very little mechanical understanding. If you buy this car without any further investigation of the mechanical stability than you are what this proverb considers the fool.

If you are of the mind to see both the exterior quality of the vehicle and all the way through to the inner mechanical workings, understanding

Marshmallow Chips −*" The Sweetest Chip With the Saltiest Flavor"* implications of all of this for subtle aspects of your life past, present, and future, and if you connect your wisdom about the car with your understanding of the world around you, and make your decision based on this thorough inspection, you are considered the wise man in this proverb.

He whose face gives no light shall never become a star.

–William Blake

If you are not positive about life than you will never do anything with it. You won't shine like a star! You must also give or share that positivity with others.

Marshmallow Chips – *" The Sweetest Chip With the Saltiest Flavor"*

Eternity is in love with the productions of time.

—William Blake

Our eternal souls that live in the finite human body are in love with things that are created or happen during the limited life span of ones term on earth. For instance we all congratulate those who become famous or invent something or find a cure. These are the things we are in love with as they happen. When Alexander Fleming found penicillin or Oppenheimer created the atom bomb. We all awe and marvel at the productions of the human mind.

From nature's perspective eternity has been producing flowers over and over again.
  Eternity itself must be in love with this finite creation because it continues to produce it.

Marshmallow Chips — *" The Sweetest Chip With the Saltiest Flavor"*

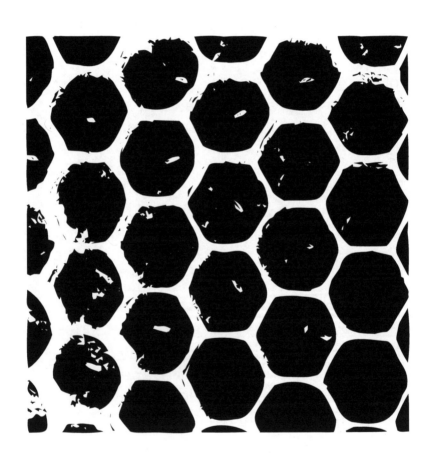

The busy bee has no time for sorrow.

—William Blake

When you stay busy and your attention is always focused on the next task or place to go you have very little time to sit back and reflect on how miserable the reality of your existence really is. Instead you just stay busy enough so that you don't even have the time to ponder it.

Example:

My puppy is beautiful. We go for walks every afternoon. Yesterday my puppy got run over by an 18 wheeler. I cried.

My work life is really busy. Soon after the tragic event I had to return to work and continue to dominate the stock market floor with all the other traders.

Though the loss of my puppy is sorrowful, there is no way I could compete at my job and think about how sad my loss is.

The hours of folly are measured by the clock, but of wisdom: no clock can measure.

–William Blake

When we make mistakes their impact can easily be measured in the physical world of material things, space, and time.. We can say to ourselves " Yes from this time to that I was unaware of (example) so I continued to fail at (example)" Things began to improve once I figured (Example) out.

Wisdom is a deep realization , understanding or insight into the nature of our world or existence. When you deepen your wisdom than the effect of it on your perception is impossible to measure because it can change how you see even yourself and how you interpret the truth.

Marshmallow Chips – " *The Sweetest Chip With the Saltiest Flavor"*

All wholesome food is caught without a net or a trap.

–William Blake

This must have a moral standard for taking the life of an animal in order to nourish ones self. Because you did not have to perform the act of killing another living creature you have remained in the wholesome state.

Bring out number weight and measure in year of dearth.

–William Blake

Dearth refers to the very tough times in life like the recession of 1927. People were lining up in the middle of the streets to eat soup from the food line. It is important that in these times you measure carefully your finances and or valuables such as food or things that could be traded for other things you might need. Take into account all the things you have and own so that you are not careless with maintaining your survival.

Marshmallow Chips – *" The Sweetest Chip With the Saltiest Flavor"*

No bird soars too high, if he soars with his own wings.

–William Blake

If you reach great heights in your profession and take on tasks that are beyond your ability to complete on your own, but instead succeed because you have friends who are qualified to help you complete the tasks that are too difficult for you, then you are not flying with your own wings. If your friends should suddenly desert you for some reason, or simply become unavailable, maybe because of death, and you are left alone to complete the tasks that were originally bestowed just upon you to complete you will fail miserably without their help. Your pretensions will be shown to the world. You will fall from the sky.

If on the other hand you take responsibility for your own abilities and only go for what you honestly feel your own self capable, than you are flying with your own wings and you have confidence in yourself while always keeping an eye on your own limitations. Try not to exceed them inappropriately to the point that you will fail.

Marshmallow Chips – *" The Sweetest Chip With the Saltiest Flavor"*

A dead body revenges not injuries.

−William Blake

Anyone who dies because of the actions of another will not be able to revenge injury upon the person who caused their death because they are dead.

Marshmallow Chips −" *The Sweetest Chip With the Saltiest Flavor"*

> *The most sublime act is to set another before you.*
>
> –William Blake

The greatest thing you can do is to use your own talents and skills to help your fellow man or woman in their own struggle. Help someone and put "them" before "you".

Example:

I met a girl who was living in a homeless shelter. She was very pretty and I wondered why is this beautiful girl in a homeless shelter? Also, when I began talking with her I noticed she was very intelligent.

I was very, very busy with many responsibilities of my own at the time, but I felt drawn to help this person.

This made me begin to think with even greater curiosity "How is this person in such a bad place?".

Turns out she was mugged outside her apartment. The bad guys beat her up and threw her into a dumpster. She was then taken to the hospital for her injuries. She was then placed in the Psych ward to help her

recover mentally. She spent months in hospitals. During this whole time she suffered amnesia from getting hit over the head. She had also been evicted from her apartment and all of her things had been sold to Goodwill.

As I got to know her, I began to see and understand her current state more clearly and decided I would like to help this young woman put her life back together.

I dropped all my own responsibilities to help her immediately. I wanted to see her liberated from this difficult situation. Like John the Baptist with Jesus, I said, "She must increase".

Since she was a very capable person already, just lacking fundamentals like a job and place to live, I could see her confidence was lacking because of her past experiences she just needed some rejuvenation.

I found her a weekend job. I helped her apply for some really good jobs making over $40,000 a year. She has a degree and 4.0 grade average so I thought, "This should be easy". We looked together for apartments online and found some that might work for her.
Her life improved with my care. This is the most sublime act:

Put someone else before yourself using your own position of power or insight to improve them.

Marshmallow Chips – "*The Sweetest Chip With the Saltiest Flavor*"

> *If the fool would persist in his folly he would become wise.*
>
> –William Blake

Starting to reflect about Blake's idea of excess and persistence - it is a theme that we see again and again in his work - in a sense about the real Way of things and not hindering with ego or fear based prudence leading to sincere experience, wisdom, unification

Example:

When a young man has a few too many alcoholic beverages, gets drunk and of course has a smashing good time but then wakes up in the morning vomiting and feeling absolutely wretched he begins to ponder the process of his actions.

Get drunk equals hang over. So the young buck over many nights of partying learning the same lesson starts to pace his consumption of alcohol knowing to drink in moderation and save his brain for the following morning. That is real wisdom!

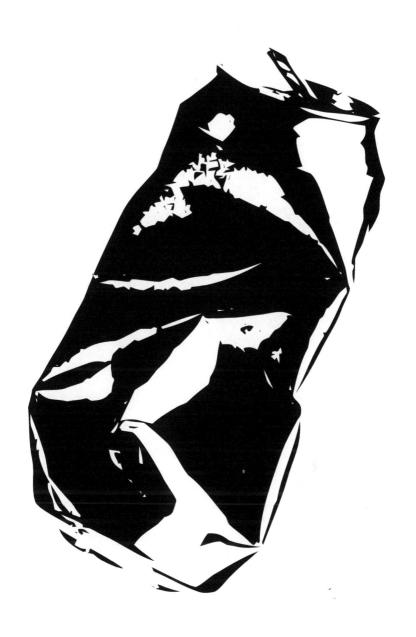

Marshmallow Chips – " *The Sweetest Chip With the Saltiest Flavor"*

Folly is the cloak of knavery.

−William Blake

Hiding is "Cloaking" and "Knavery" is dishonesty. Beware of people who appear to make fools of themselves or make too many mistakes, because it is possible they are using these mistakes to disguise some devious plan.

Marshmallow Chips – "*The Sweetest Chip With the Saltiest Flavor"*

Shame is prides cloak.

—William Blake

People hide their pride with shame. A person feeling shame is expressing injury to something that they feel great pride in.

Example:

A person is born into a family of many brothers and sisters who grow up to be successful professionals of high standing (doctors, lawyers etc.). This person always told everyone growing up that he was going to be a famous actor. She spent her life acting in many plays and films. Unfortunately by way of circumstance and skill level they did not become a famous actor. Every time this person is around his brothers and sisters he feels ashamed and hates that his nieces and nephews might think that he is a stupid loser.

The reason this person is feeling ashamed is because he or she has so much pride in their talent. Now they feel shame because their ego has not been fulfilled but they still must meet with their family members and face their failure.

Marshmallow Chips –" *The Sweetest Chip With the Saltiest Flavor"*

*Prisons are built with stones of law,
Brothels with bricks of religion.*

–William Blake

The law that we govern our people with is the prison of which we live in. The law determines whether or not you are allowed to cross a street if a traffic light says you can. If you break the laws you get sent to prison confined to a cell built with stones.

Religion is moral law that praises you when you follow its moral standards. A brothel is a place where the opposite of the Religious moral standard takes place. It is a place we enter willingly unlike the prisons built with stones. Because we have created a moral standard/law with religion the causal effect of all we distain morally still needs a place to exist and so brothels are created. Brothels are used for things like sex out of wedlock. A place created to feed your lust and commit the unholy desires we hide from others.

Marshmallow Chips – "*The Sweetest Chip With the Saltiest Flavor*"

The pride of the peacock is the glory of god.

–William Blake

William Blake uses different animals as symbols of certain characteristics of God. The peacock struts its feathers with radiant beauty like a shimmering gem. All its feathers are iridescent and beautiful. The bird itself is no bigger than a small turkey but when the feathers are raised and its beauty is shown it not only provides an illusion of being larger in size to its prey for defense but its very nature when in full bloom is very proud, beautiful, radiant and glorious, so it has become the signature of the very nature of pride as an archetype.

Since medieval times the peacock was seen as a symbol of Christ's immortality.

Marshmallow Chips – *" The Sweetest Chip With the Saltiest Flavor"*

The lust of the goat is the bounty of God.

–*William Blake*

The goat represents the symbol of lust in all of us. Since the goat is especially sexual he becomes the signature for reproduction. That feeling of lust is what drives the forces of God's creation. It is the bounty of God because it produces all the new animal life or all life for that matter. Its desire and drive powers all creation in the Universe.

Marshmallow Chips – "*The Sweetest Chip With the Saltiest Flavor*"

The wrath of the lion is the wisdom of God.

–William Blake

When the leader (The Lion) of a group or community, nation is brought to anger by a circumstance that they react to with rage, this rage comes from being concerned for the group because that is the leader's job. They do this because as the leader they know when their plans for harmony are being compromised by something. They bring wrath upon this compromising element to overcome it and continue their plans for continued harmony and progress. In many religious texts it is also described how God becomes wrathful when stupid or evil humans disrupt goodness and harmony, so there are places where anger and wrath can be wise - when the well being of the group or all of Humanity is at stake.

Marshmallow Chips – "*The Sweetest Chip With the Saltiest Flavor*"

The nakedness of woman is the work of God.

–William Blake

The nakedness of woman is God's masterpiece, his truly most beautiful creation. His artwork. For our species to continue the woman must be the most beautiful thing we desire.

Example:

If you were to see the great works of Michelangelo and you thought "Oh my! That is beautiful artwork"

Someone turns to you and says" Yup, that is Michelangelo".

When you turn and see a woman disrobed, you are viewing the art of God.
And again you say "Oh my!" and someone turns to you and say's "That is the work of God".

Marshmallow Chips – "*The Sweetest Chip With the Saltiest Flavor*"

Excess of sorrow laughs, Excess of joy weeps.

—William Blake

When you begin to cry and it turns into extreme wailing suddenly your expression changes into laughter as a natural phenomenon. Blake wants to help us understand that anything in its excess will often quickly change into its opposite.

Sorrow Example:

You are driving down the road and suddenly your car tire blows out, you hit a guardrail, then you get out to fix it and a seagull drops poop on your head, your boss calls you and says " where are you?" He fires you because you're late. While you are fixing the tire you see your girlfriend pass by in a car with a man you have never seen before. You throw your hands up and begin to laugh. What could possibly be next you think? Ha! Suddenly you feel a toothache.

Joy Example:

When you become over excited from laughing you will begin to cry but not because you are sad.

You are working in an artificial crab packing facility. You are working with people who like to throw fish slime at you on "accident".

It is time for lunch break. You go to the local convenience store and you purchase a scratch ticket and win $250,000. Can you believe it?!!! Then suddenly you look outside and see your coworkers getting fired for their indecent

Marshmallow Chips –" *The Sweetest Chip With the Saltiest Flavor"*

behavior. When you begin to walk back to your work facility, your supervisor quickly confronts you and says "we are promoting you to facilities manager and your pay will double".

Then suddenly you receive a call from your long lost boyfriend from high school who just wants to tell you that he loves you and wants to see you. Besides pinching yourself as hard as you possibly can because this seems so unbelievable and unreal you begin to laugh and the power of all the joy overcomes you and you begin to sob and wail with tremendous joy.

Marshmallow Chips – "*The Sweetest Chip With the Saltiest Flavor*"

The roaring of lions, the howling of wolves, the raging of the stormy sea, and the destructive sword, are portions of eternity too great for the eye of man.

–William Blake

On the surface we can perceive these things. You read the proverb and images may come to mind for each of these topics.

Each one of these things are indicators pointing to things that go beyond the borders of our comprehension. The awesome wildness of reality is something being pointed at. The stormy sea is out of man's control and what will happen with the changes of the sea are so constant we can not really comprehend it. The destructive sword is out of our comprehension because we don't know what happens after we die and no one knows who will win the battle. This points to the border of our human perception of reality.

Marshmallow Chips – "*The Sweetest Chip With the Saltiest Flavor*"

The fox condemns the trap not himself.

–William Blake

The fox is the type of person to believe that his clever and cunning abilities will allow him to navigate through all situations. When he reaches a point where he has been captured by others he refuses to acknowledge his own actions and reflect as to what he himself might be doing wrong. Instead he blames the people or the trap that he is caught in.

Marshmallow Chips – "*The Sweetest Chip With the Saltiest Flavor*"

Joys impregnate. Sorrows bring forth.

—William Blake

When good things happen to you they instill a confidence and maybe even an ego. You have been impregnated by the joy. You are happy and fat like the Buddha after a picnic. You are full with the joy! Also you might be pregnant because you were sharing so much joy with your lover.

When you have sorrows you do all that you can to improve the situation so as not to feel so awful. The acts of the things you do are the bringing forth spoken of in this proverb.

Also if you are pregnant than sorrows of pain are about to bring forth a little baby.

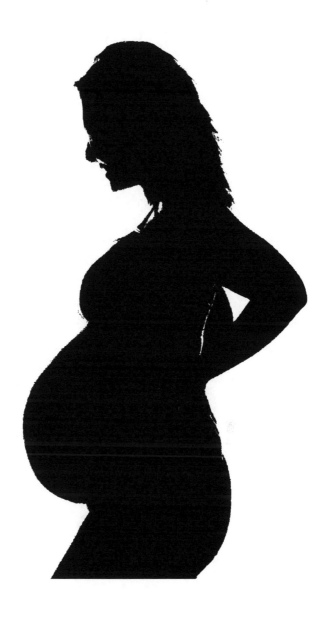

Marshmallow Chips – "*The Sweetest Chip With the Saltiest Flavor*"

Let man wear the fell of the lion. Woman the fleece of a sheep.

–William Blake

Let the sexes be of the nature the people in the east call yin and yang. Yin is the female receptive and Yang the Male Aggressor.

I believe one can also say about this that one is that it is about being open and honest - as opposed to the points about cloaks - it is about shining forth as who you actually are and not being sneaky and hiding behind a cloak.

Marshmallow Chips – "*The Sweetest Chip With the Saltiest Flavor*"

The bird a nest, the spider a web, man friendship

—William Blake

The bird's nest is its home. The spider's web is a spider's home. Man or woman's interconnectedness with other individuals he or she considers friends is his or her home.

Marshmallow Chips – "*The Sweetest Chip With the Saltiest Flavor*"

> *The selfish smiling fool, & the sullen frowning fool, shall be both thought wise, that they may be a rod.*
>
> –William Blake

Both thought wise to be a rod meaning each are one of the opposite spectrums of human emotion and thought wise because they are one in the same. One emotion cannot be considered wise and the other not because we use both to express ourselves depending on situation or circumstance.

A rod in biblical writings was something a sheepherder carried with him to protect himself and to fight with.

So if you are in a business arrangement or competition and you come out on top. You find the path to success quicker than the other person or company. You smile with your selfishness , you are winning.

The competitors are not smiling at this point. They are frowning. It is tough to be on losing side. Thankfully when we see it as a rod, even when we are on the losing side when know the scales will tip in our favor again.

You know it as a rod now. The spectrum of emotions become less personal and more objectified with in yourself.

Marshmallow Chips –" *The Sweetest Chip With the Saltiest Flavor"*

> *What is now proved was once, only imagin'd.*
>
> −William Blake

Leonardo Da Vinci. There he is again imagining the future. Trying to figure out how birds take flight. He is fascinated by the idea that man himself can figure out how to fly.

After many attempts by lots of creative ambitious people, the success according to history of flight takes off with the Wright Brothers.

Now when you are sitting in a commercial airliner and enjoying your meal, prepared for you by your flight steward, you can try to imagine what it was like to even ponder the possibility of human beings before the Wright Brothers, people of the past "imagining" flying 5 miles above the surface of the earth, eating a lobster roll, served by a person standing comfortably next to them.

Marshmallow Chips – "*The Sweetest Chip With the Saltiest Flavor*"

The rat, the mouse, the fox, the rabbit: watch the roots; the lion, the tiger, the horse, the elephant, watch the fruits.

—William Blake

The rat, the mouse and the fox are a symbol for "paid employees" in the socio-economic structure of how the people in our system feed. They are working for the Lions the Tigers, Horses and Elephants who are watching the fruits (Owners of established business).

Marshmallow Chips – "*The Sweetest Chip With the Saltiest Flavor*"

The cistern contains; the fountain overflows.

—William Blake

Cistern:

When people learn information about a trade they begin to acquire knowledge. They learn the rules of the trade and its nature, skill set, and so forth. They eventually master the specific trade. They have all the experience and information about the trade inside of them now. Many people who have acquired the knowledge and secrets of a trade do not share the information. A person such as this would be considered a Cistern in this proverb. They fear that by releasing the information they would lose potential business and create competition.

Fountain:

Being like a fountain that overflows means that you become a conduit and allow the information you have learned to pass through you freely to other interested parties. The nature of this way allows your mind a sense of abundance and freedom that being a cistern does not. Because you are not attached to anything there are no walls to cage your own mind. Teachers are often found having this type of mind.

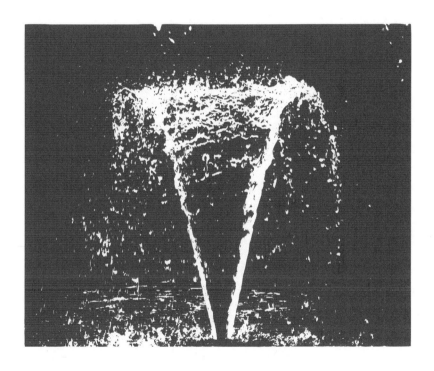

Marshmallow Chips – *"The Sweetest Chip With the Saltiest Flavor"*

One thought fills immensity

–William Blake

Before you have a thought in the quiet of your mind there is nothing. When you have a thought it is like the rising sun over the horizon shining all its rays of light filling the whole of your mind's attention. Your mind is completely filled with an idea.

At a larger scale….one thought can fill the entire world. Everyone is experiencing this single thought.

Example:

When Sputnik was first set into orbit it was on everyone's mind. Then came the race to the moon. The idea of walking on the moon captured everyone's imagination.

Marshmallow Chips – "*The Sweetest Chip With the Saltiest Flavor*"

Always be ready to speak your mind and a base man will avoid you.

–William Blake

A base man is someone who is acts with little care or concern for the principles and codes of morality, spirituality.

Example:

You are at a party and everyone is having a drink and listening to music. They are talking about the difference between walnuts and peanuts. One of the guests make a racist comment stating that Black people are more like walnuts and white people are like peanuts.

First thing that happens is, everyone at the party draws a blank and wonders, "how does that make sense?" Then they realize that even if it did not make sense it was racist and some of them start to become uncomfortable.

Suddenly this guy named "Joe" shows up to the party and all the men and woman there know Joe for being a stand up guy who calls it

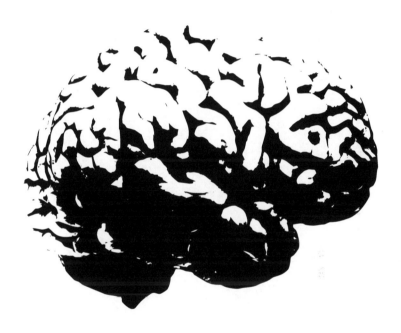

Marshmallow Chips – *" The Sweetest Chip With the Saltiest Flavor"*

like he sees it and always has respect for equality and honesty, integrity in the world.

The guy who made the racist nut joke is worried about his expressions around Joe because his expressions are not of the collective higher moral standard and are considered base....so he avoids Joe.

Everything possible to be believed is an image of truth.

–William Blake

The world is only limited by the expanse of our own imaginations. Truth is as broad or deep as our imagination. That is why Einstein said, " Imagination is more important than knowledge".

Knowledge is an account of all that we already know about a subject or life altogether. We've already "been there done that" if we know something.

The imagination produces new creative possibilities for the thinking mind to follow afterwards and discover. This has allowed us to make world-shattering things like the wheel, spaceships, cell phones and real dragons. Yes real dragons!!

We think we have only imagined dragons in legend. The truth is that they are becoming real now! We are becoming more knowledgeable of genetics, the genome, and how to manipulate life in order to create never-seen-before creatures. The dragon is one of them.

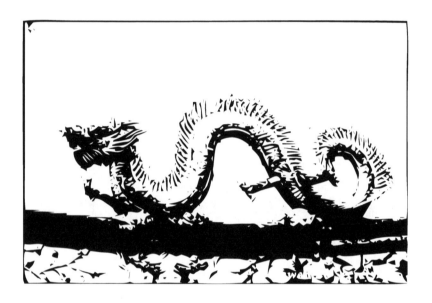

Now the dragon and the cell phone both started out similarly. First we were watching Star Trek and communicators, and now we are living day in and day out with this thing that was only imagined first "The cell phone".

We imagined dragons a long time ago but the technology is finally coming around to produce them. Far fetched? It is not. It is all possible. Even Aliens folks.

All the different possibilities that the world offers you to think about are representations or manifestations of what this world is, because you are thinking about them. They are the world. They are the part of the truth. So if you are thinking about Aliens or God in the sky or anything else in your imagination you are dealing with the truth regardless of whatever you are thinking about.

Marshmallow Chips – " *The Sweetest Chip With the Saltiest Flavor"*

The Eagle never lost so much time as to learn of the crow.

−William Blake

The mind and consciousness of someone who has not yet really considered their own death lives in the mind of the eagle. They are invincible and free from the concept of dying or an end. They live in a state of eternity without the great consequence.

The eagle represents someone who has not considered his own end. The crow is a symbol for death. When the Eagle learns of the crow he learns about his own death. When he learns this it is a loss of time because the true genius sees through the eyes of eternity. That the end is all a part of the everything. When you start worrying about your own death you are wasting your time.

Marshmallow Chips – *"The Sweetest Chip With the Saltiest Flavor"*

> *The fox provides for himself, but God provides for the lion.*
>
> –William Blake

Fox:

The fox is a person who is self-centered and interacts with the world doing everything for his own personal gain.

Lion:

The Lion is someone who is communally based, and his or her actions stem from the perspective of a group. Since the Lion's needs are greater than his own self, God provides for him. The Lion is the King/Leader. The Lion must have faith in a higher power for all things to work out.

Marshmallow Chips – "*The Sweetest Chip With the Saltiest Flavor*"

Think in the morning. Act in the noon. Eat in the evening. Sleep in the night.

—William Blake

William Blake apparently felt like this rhythm was the most preferable for approaching the day.

Marshmallow Chips – "*The Sweetest Chip With the Saltiest Flavor*"

He who has suffered you to impose on him knows you.

−William Blake

When you have been put in a situation in which you had to reach out to others for help, your own true self is seen because you must overcome pride in order to be able to expose your own helplessness. Those who help you know you because they see you in a way that others might never experience. Your times might be better in other situations and the depth of your desperation can't be reenacted because your ego is too strong. Desperation often brings out your most humble nature, and if this is shared with another who helps you they see into this great humility and come to know you because of it; they know you free of pretension.

Marshmallow Chips – *" The Sweetest Chip With the Saltiest Flavor"*

As the plow follows words, so God rewards prayers.

—William Blake

The plow is literally directed by someone yelling out to their mule "hyaahh!" and then maybe cracking a whip if the mule is stubborn. The mule will continue on and the field will be plowed. Work is physically accomplished this way.

If you pray to God for what is truly your heart's desire, He will reward you with what you desire because if you truly want something and you put all your heart and soul into it your being begins to change itself from within to direct itself with the most progressive possibilities for making it come true. Which is the relationship of your inner world communicating with god and how your prayers find their rewards.

Marshmallow Chips – *"The Sweetest Chip With the Saltiest Flavor"*

The tygers of wrath are wiser than the horses of instruction.

–William Blake

The horses of instruction are the teachers of institutions. They have learned books and trained to teach but they are not the same as a Tyger of wrath. Horses are patient, dutiful; they do their work loyally.

A tyger of wrath is someone who is entirely balls to the wall, boldly taking hold of life and is not teaching but advancing with their own wisdom throughout every circumstance life presents them with.

Marshmallow Chips – " *The Sweetest Chip With the Saltiest Flavor"*

Expect poison from the standing water.

−William Blake

Quite literally standing water produces all sorts of bacteria, which causes many human illnesses. Thankfully we now have penicillin to defend against the tyranny of bacteria.

This can also be interpreted as times of no movement, of stagnation in human affairs. Things have come to a standstill within a group and the fear is that poison may result. You must expect it and be prepared for it.

Marshmallow Chips – "*The Sweetest Chip With the Saltiest Flavor*"

You never know what is enough unless you know what is more than enough.

–William Blake

Very much like Goldie Locks and the three bears when she chooses the right temperature porridge.

Example:

If you have a client for your gardening business and they tell a friend about your services. That friend calls you and wants to hire you. You say, "Ok Great!"

After the new client sees your work on their garden another one of their friends calls you and wants to hire you.

You are only one person in this case. You can only manage so many properties in an 8 to 10 hour day working. Eventually you have more than you can handle. You then realize that by yourself you can do only 3 properties a day.

Exceeding what you can handle allows you to become wise to your own limitations.

Marshmallow Chips – "*The Sweetest Chip With the Saltiest Flavor*"

Listen to the fools reproach. It is a kingly title!

–William Blake

If you are a truly unique individual approaching life the way you like to and small minded people berate you with criticism than it is actually a compliment and a kingly title because they themselves are fools just following along with what everyone else has told them is the way to be and because you are different and they criticize you out of not understanding you, it means you are beyond them. You are kingly amongst their view of the world.

Marshmallow Chips – *"The Sweetest Chip With the Saltiest Flavor"*

> *The eyes of fire, the nostrils of air, the mouth of water, the beard of earth.*
>
> –William Blake

This refers to oneness with life and characterizes that we are of earth. This is a helpful koan:

"Does sound go to the ear or does the ear go to sound?"

Eyes of Fire:
The soul or the light of your being is in your eyes and so our eyes are like the fire of earth. It is possible to see the difference between a dead human being and a live one. If you were dead the light within your eyes would be out.

Nostrils of Air:
Nostrils are constantly breathing in and out the air and if you take the time to just breathe you will feel the air of earth.

Mouth of Water:
Sit for a moment and keep your mouth closed. Don't swallow and notice that your mouth begins to fill with water. This is the water of earth filling up in your mouth.

Beard of Earth:
The beard of your face is like the trees that grow on the crust of the earth. Trees are the earth's beard.

Marshmallow Chips – *" The Sweetest Chip With the Saltiest Flavor"*

The weak in courage are strong in cunning

—William Blake

People who lack courage are very good at taking underhanded devious actions to screw you over.

Marshmallow Chips – " *The Sweetest Chip With the Saltiest Flavor"*

The apple tree never asks the Beech how he shall grow, nor the lion, the horse, how he shall take his prey.

–William Blake

Mastery. You are, at the end of all things standing alone. You are left with the responsibility of choosing for the benefit of your own destiny and the destiny of the lives around you. You choose what will be best. You do not have to ask another for direction. Especially if you are an apple tree producing fruit and asking a Beech tree which produces no fruit. A horse is certainly not going to help you if you are a lion on how to take prey. To look into the very nature of a creation is amazing. How each different type of being uniquely responds or adapts based on its own essence and characteristics.

Trust in your own nature. What your own nature tells you.

Another angle might be this: this proverb is a celebration of the diversity of the forms of Life found in all Creation.

The thankful receiver bears a plentiful harvest.

–William Blake

Showing gratitude for someone else's gracious behavior or for the gifts of God or nature magnifies the experience 10 fold.

Marshmallow Chips – *" The Sweetest Chip With the Saltiest Flavor"*

If others had not been foolish we should be so.

–William Blake

Everything is good, goodness encompasses success or failure. Even when you do something stupid you are giving a gift to others.

Example:

In 1844 when everybody was listening to "Christy's Melodies" and partying like foolish teenagers, nitrous oxide was a party favor. One gentleman imbued with innate curiosity for all things debauchery took too much of the gas. He was to perform at the laughing gas stage show that night and when he did he accidentally brushed his leg on the stage and cut his leg wide open. What was to be marveled at that night was that he didn't even realize that he had gashed his leg and people had to tell him " OMG your leg dear sir!".

As a result Nitrous oxide became an early form of anesthesia.

Marshmallow Chips – *" The Sweetest Chip With the Saltiest Flavor"*

Second Example:

When Columbus was to make his voyage to the Americas across the Atlantic, people told him that was crazy, foolish and stupid.

"The world is flat and you will just fall off the edge." They touted.

Columbus was acting foolish to other but look what he discovered. If he had not been foolish we would not know so many new things.

Marshmallow Chips – *"The Sweetest Chip With the Saltiest Flavor"*

The soul of sweet delight can never be defiled.

—William Blake

The soul of sweet delight is an archetype signature of manifestation that can never be defiled. What is "an archetype signature of manifestation"? Is this meaning that the soul of sweet delight is one of our core feelings when we are manifesting something from the core? Yes I believe it does.

Example:

Someone close to you dies. It could be your mother. You will feel incredible loss and mourn for her for a certain period of time. This feeling and period of expression is known as "mourning". It is a signature feeling that others recognize when they observe it.

The soul of sweet delight is also a signature but something much more fun to experience than mourning. The soul of sweet delight is like a dream where you are so happy with your life that everything appears to be like magic. Your heart is so perfect in its love it cannot be defiled.

Someone suddenly yells out of their car "Loser" as they pass by and it doesn't even touch your mood or the quality of your experience. You just watch them pass by yelling "Loser" and that's it.

Marshmallow Chips – *" The Sweetest Chip With the Saltiest Flavor"*

When thou seest an eagle, thou seest a portion of genius, lift up thy head!

−William Blake

When you see someone who is without fear and the concept of death in their consciousness, this is a portion of genius. This is a trace of the characteristics that are commonly associated with people of genius.

These traits are signatures of the personality of a genius. Seeing eternity and that the end of anything is only a part of everything, so there really is no end or beginning. Consider this well.

Marshmallow Chips −" *The Sweetest Chip With the Saltiest Flavor*"

As the caterpillar chooses the fairest leaves to lay her eggs on, so the priest lays his curse on the fairest joys.

–William Blake

A caterpillar finds the fairest leaves to nourish her new baby eggs with. The fairest will provide the most nutrients.

A priest lays his curse on the fairest joys as it is to him the greatest sacrifice and sign of self-control/mastery. This type of curse leads to spiritual fulfillment for him. This is a type of nutrient. One for spiritual fulfillment (priest) and the other to nourish the body (caterpillar).

Marshmallow Chips – *" The Sweetest Chip With the Saltiest Flavor"*

To create a little flower is the labor of ages.

−William Blake

It takes forever to become your full potential. The flower is a symbol for your full potential.

Marshmallow Chips −" *The Sweetest Chip With the Saltiest Flavor"*

Damn, braces: Bless relaxes.

−William Blake

When times have you stuck and there is nothing you can do to get out of it you damn that situation because it is awful.

When things are stress free and wonderful you bless those times.

Marshmallow Chips − *" The Sweetest Chip With the Saltiest Flavor"*

The best wine is the oldest the best water the newest.

–William Blake

Wine:

Over time the special blend of ingredients that make up wine begin to harmonize and produce a quality flavor and aroma. This becomes a great value to many who love the tastes of fine wine.

Just like wine a human life can be seen to age with subtle perfection, creating a full and rich understanding and presence of life.

Let's use the master carpenter for example. When he was just a boy his father gave him a hammer and saw for his birthday. The boy built a fun little tree house in the backyard of their home high in the tall branches. Of course building the tree house was fun but the father saw his son had not put enough supports on the platform of the tree house.

The father congratulated the boy for his efforts but soon told him to take it down because it was too dangerous.

Marshmallow Chips – *" The Sweetest Chip With the Saltiest Flavor"*

The boy cried and threw a tantrum, yelling out "It is not fair!".

The father let the boy have his fit an when the fort was completely taken down the father brought out his own hammer and saw and told the boy "Let us work together for a while and I will show you how to build a real tree house".

The boy was so excited!! He danced and sang. He and his father built a great tree house that all the other children loved to play on for years.

For many years the boy's father trained him in the ways of the master carpenter. When the boy became a man his fellow citizens revered him as the greatest carpenter in the land.

The middle aged successful carpenter received a phone call one day.

"Your father died while eating cherries. He choked on one of the hard pits." A voice whispered through the handset.

The carpenter wept and felt an extreme pain and feelings of loss.

The young man now master carpenter built many fine homes in their village. He was the pride f his father and all his family.

Now that his father, whom he loved is dead he digs deep into his soul to figure out what he could make to truly honor him.

Though the talents of the carpenter do not free him from the treacheries of loss in this life, but provide the fine ingredients of all his experience that now have prepared him for this great work ahead.

He builds the most magnificent tomb anyone has every laid eye upon. It is adorned with meaning so deep and skill so wonderful, each walks away with an elevated glow.

Marshmallow Chips –" *The Sweetest Chip With the Saltiest Flavor"*

Water:

Water straight from the spring has not had time to be affected by the air from sitting in a jug or tub. The earth through many sedimentary layers filters the water from a spring. It has many minerals in it because of its natural filtration process. This is why the water that is freshest is the best. If it had been sitting over time it begins to grow bacteria that causes illness.

A student who does not have a history or knowledge of a given subject to be taught is most open and ready to learn with the attitude that he truly does not know and wishes to learn. This makes his mind the freshest.

Marshmallow Chips – "*The Sweetest Chip With the Saltiest Flavor*"

Prayers plow not! Sorrows weep not!

–William Blake

You cannot expect the things you want to get done just by praying for them. The plow is a symbol for getting things done. The farmer plows a field and plants his seeds and so a bountiful harvest is had for his hard work. He cannot just stand near the field and pray for it to grow corn if he does not actually go out there and plant it himself.

If you don't actually mourn and let your emotions out in relationship to what is bothering you than it will just stay in you as sorrow.

Marshmallow Chips – "*The Sweetest Chip With the Saltiest Flavor*"

> *The head sublime, the heart Pathos, the genitals Beauty, the hands & feet proportion.*
>
> –William Blake

Head Sublime: The head is responsible for visions, thinking, calculating. With it you can awe inspire those around you with your own thoughts….

Heart Pathos: The heart is a compassionate organ evoking sympathy, empathy and pity.

Genitals Beauty: The genitals are beautiful because they don't think but feel amazing and do nothing but inspire incredible sensations.

Hands and Feet Proportion: As we have seen the many reproductions of Leonardo DaVinci proportion drawing of a man in a circle with arms and legs outstretched.

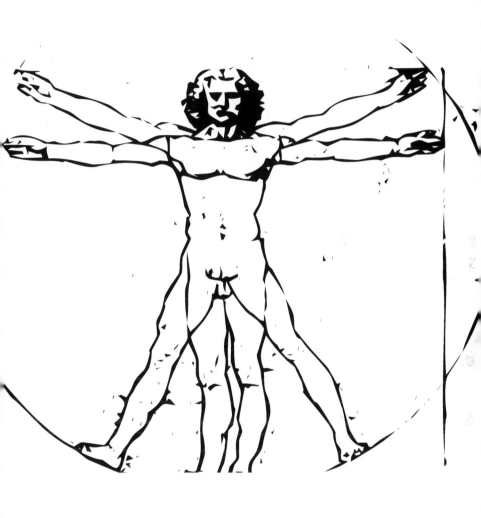

Marshmallow Chips – "*The Sweetest Chip With the Saltiest Flavor*"

As the air to a bird of the sea to a fish, so is contempt to the contemptible.

–William Blake

When you hold contempt in this world for another person, life itself or for your relatives, that contempt actually begins to surround your inner world/thinking and filters all that you do distorting your very existence with contempt. The bird and the air exist together in mutual partnership balanced. The fish also must have the sea and it is also dependent and encapsulated by it.

Someone who is contemptible is someone who does disgraceful things. They cannot be respected or honored because their actions don't merit such rewards. So everyone has contempt for them. If our world is a psycho environment, collectively people will begin to share the opinion that you are contemptible and you will be surrounded like water for a fish or air for a bird with the contempt of others. Contemptible people end up surrounded by contempt. And so the people who are holding the world in contempt are not only viewing the world from how they feel and think internally in a contemptuous way but also the world also holds them in contempt.

Marshmallow Chips – "*The Sweetest Chip With the Saltiest Flavor*"

Example:

Hitler was held in contempt by most of the modern world of the early 1900's. He did many things people did not agree with and so he was surrounded by contempt and most people did all that they could to eventually put an end to his tyranny.

Hitler was also very upset young man for not being accepted to art school. He believed himself to be an amazing artist and when that wasn't the way the world responded to him he started to feel contempt from within about the whole world.

Marshmallow Chips – "*The Sweetest Chip With the Saltiest Flavor*"

The crow wish'd everything was black, the owl, that everything was white.

–William Blake

At the furthest point back in your consciousness there is a dial that can be at a setting somewhere in between "I love God and all of life at one end" and at the other "I despise God to the very core of my existence and everything in this life".

The owl represents the person who loves God at his core. The Crow despises God and his perspective is to hate the world and everyone in it.

Marshmallow Chips – "*The Sweetest Chip With the Saltiest Flavor*"

Exuberance is beauty.

—William Blake

Exuberance means being full of energy, excitement and cheerfulness. This state of being like this is beautiful especially when it is you experiencing it.

Marshmallow Chips – "*The Sweetest Chip With the Saltiest Flavor*"

If the lion was advised by the fox, he would be cunning.

—William Blake

The Lion is the king. He is a ruler. He comes from a place where keeping order and maintaining the good of his kingdom are of first priority. Honor and order are the codes for the lion.

The fox is cunning. When a fox wants to take her prey, she will dance around in front of it doing backflips and wave her tail. The fox entertains her prey until it is hypnotized by the performance.

So let's say that the Lion was inclined to overtake another country. If he was advised by the fox she would show him ways of tricking the enemy and winning victory.

Marshmallow Chips – "*The Sweetest Chip With the Saltiest Flavor*"

Improvement makes straight roads, but the crooked roads without improvement are roads of genius.

—William Blake

When a person is given a path by the people that are born before him like parents and they start saying " You must have a home, Self respect, a good job, always brush your teeth, wear respectable clothing and marry a nice girl".

A person will take this advice and organize their goals and actions to attain these things. In the process of attaining these goals it is important that you maintain a certain amount of order and discipline to keep what you have and save for what you want, so you can improve. These are straight roads.

When a person is going with the flow and one week they are doing great and the next they will be homeless it is not a big problem to them. They are ready to experience the crooked path and are not too attached to a standard of living set by the social normative of their time. Plus there is a great amount of freedom to belonging to the moment and always something new to learn. By always being ready to change and adapt to new

Environments you learn a great deal about life and how things work.

"Adapt or Die" -United States Marine Corps Slogan.

Also no one really knows where the road less taken will lead. This ultimately makes for the most creative path.

Marshmallow Chips – " *The Sweetest Chip With the Saltiest Flavor* "

Sooner murder an infant in its cradle than nurse unacted desires.

−William Blake

It is better to completely rid yourself of something as soon as it develops if you are going to have to live around it and not act on it.

Example:

You are going out on a date with someone and the two of you eat at a nice restaurant and then go to the movies. The person you go out on the date with say's at the end of the date " I really enjoyed our time tonight".

You actually did not have a good time that night because you thought your date had awful breath and he was wearing a fanny pack. These are things that you could never accept in a mate but because you are a polite person you carried on with the date through to the end thinking this will be as far as I go with this person.

Now you could respond saying "it was a wonderful time for you too" but if you did that you would be nursing the unacted desire to say" I don't think we are right for each other."

Some people can nurse the unacted desire all the way to the point of marrying someone.
 The whole time they choose to be polite.
You must murder the infant in its cradle means get rid of the thing immediately that could have the potential for you to nurse something that would create an unacted desire within you like being nice to someone who is interested in you romantically but you honestly are not interested back, which would result in the unacted desire to remove yourself from the relationship.

Marshmallow Chips – "*The Sweetest Chip With the Saltiest Flavor*"

Where man is not nature is barren.

–William Blake

What I believe William Blake means by barren is unseen, uninhabited, not experienced. Because we see the world through the human experience we are limited to that specific experience. Shamans and people who are considered to have experiences beyond their human relationship to the world like shape shifting explained by many Native American tribes might be exempt.

When Nature does not have the human experience in it's recipe it is barren. It lacks the visage of a rich palate observer to enjoy it and so it is barren.

Marshmallow Chips – *" The Sweetest Chip With the Saltiest Flavor"*

> *Truth can never be told so as to be understood, and not believed.*
>
> −William Blake

Truth is and always will be subjective, because we all experience the world from individual perspectives. People collectively agree on the truth and then it becomes accepted as the truth by everyone, but really it is only believed to be the truth because we all agree that it is. It actually is not the truth. But since we collectively agree together that it is the truth, it is the truth. Once we have a truth to believe in we now have to explain it to others so they will understand what they will now agree to believe.

Example:

The Bible says that the world was created in 7 days. A lot of people believe this is the truth because a lot of people have agreed collectively that it is the truth and so they say it is truth.

Another group of people say the world was created by a Big Bang in space and that the world we live in and all the creatures evolved over millions and millions of years. A lot of people agree on this concept and so it is their truth. They believe it.

Marshmallow Chips – "*The Sweetest Chip With the Saltiest Flavor*"

Enough! Or Too much!

–William Blake

Have you had enough marshmallow chips? Or maybe, by the look of your squeamish face you might have had too much?

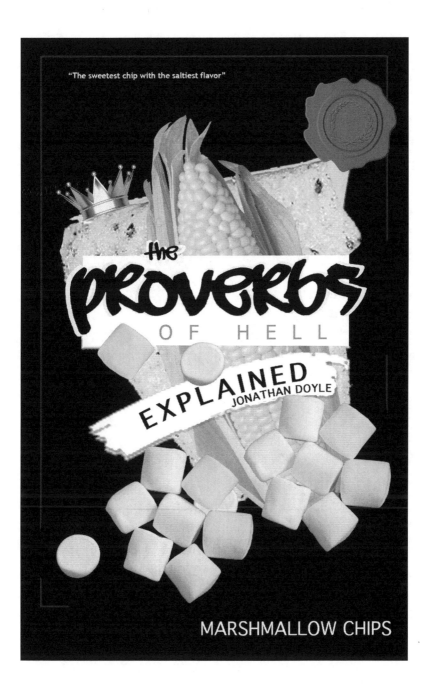

Marshmallow Chips – "*The Sweetest Chip With the Saltiest Flavor*" 157

About the Author

Jonathan Doyle grew up in the North East, deep in the hills of the New Hampshire forest. He is famous for dressing up as Bigfoot and producing short videos on Mt. Monadnock. His short videos and performances were  published in local papers causing a stir amongst the Cheshire County community. The State Park immediately investigated his activities on the mountain and deemed them a violation of park regulations and kicked him out of the park stating " Mr. Doyle will need a permit to shoot his Bigfoot videos on the mountain" Doyle fought back with the help of the American Civil Liberties Union. Doyle sued the state for $1 on grounds that his first amendment right was violated. His case made it all the way to the New Hampshire Supreme Court. The world media with publicity from such juggernauts as FOX NEWS, NPR, BBC RADIO, NEW YORK TIMES all scrambled to cover the story. Turns out Doyle was right and the Supreme Court judges decided in his favor, making Doyle the first Bigfoot performer to fight for free speech and win a dollar.

Marshmallow Chips – "*The Sweetest Chip With the Saltiest Flavor*" 159